SUNNY WAYS

RYAN FITZPATRICK

Invisible Publishing
Halifax & Toronto

Library and Archives Canada Cataloguing in Publication
Title: Sunny ways / ryan fitzpatrick.
Names: fitzpatrick, ryan, 1978- author.
Description: Poems.
Identifiers: Canadiana (print) 20220467218
              Canadiana (ebook) 20220467226
              ISBN 9781778430183 (softcover)
              ISBN 9781778430190 (EPUB)

Classification: LCC PS8611.I893 S86 2023 | DDC C811/.6—dc23

Edited by Laurie D. Graham
Cover and interior design by Megan Fildes | Typeset in Laurentian
With thanks to type designer Rod McDonald

Invisible Publishing is committed to protecting our natural environment. As part of our efforts, both the cover and interior of this book are printed on acid-free 100% post-consumer recycled fibres.

Printed and bound in Canada.

Invisible Publishing | Halifax & Toronto
www.invisiblepublishing.com

Published with the generous assistance of the Canada Council for the Arts, the Ontario Arts Council, and the Government of Canada.

  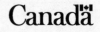

For Calgary, wherever you are

True, nature is resistant, and infinite in its depth, but it has been defeated, and now waits only for its ultimate voidance and destruction.

— Henri Lefebvre, *The Production of Space*

The air is clear, and all across Instagram – peeps are posting pics of the sunset.

— Tommy Pico, *Nature Poem*

Hibernia Mon Amour

No it will be inspiring when the sun rises over
the tankers at Kitimat but

no it will be sublime when the sun sets over
Hibernia but

no it will not be a problem after you shotgun
these tailings but

no there will absolutely be a long tail on these
historical conditions but

no you need to realize that the boom repeats
itself but

no I'm not the one who made it personal but

No these industries *should* consider them-
selves the community but

no these protestors *should* better index their
anger to the price per barrel but

no these Liberal muggers *should* get my hands
into your pockets but

no these stomachaches should *not* keep me
from work but

No there wasn't a refinery there but

no inches of topsoil trucked off somewhere but

no ducks folded into memorials but

no sky as big as Alberta but

No one can become an expert after a quick
flyover but

no the Earth should be saved before shutting
anything down but

no James Bay did send a thank you card to the
Feds but

no those ecofascists loved it when I diverted nine
free-flowing rivers to flood an area the size of
Belgium but

no those plumes flower from the faint tails of
cranes but

No I wasn't in great shape before I signed the
contract but

no the Frank Slide didn't happen but

no we may have worked there but

no we never lived there but

no we don't have to pull out but

No I find that artists are often excellent
businessmen but

no I don't find tar that I can't paint in oil but

no I don't find Smithson's *Spiral Jetty*
beautiful but

no I do find Burtynsky's scale breathtaking but

No maybe *you* should get those Robert
Bateman paintings out of City Hall but

no maybe *you* should take some prettier aerial
shots of the reclamation but

no maybe *you* should help me reclaim the
parking in front of my house but

no conclusions about the cause of the fire in
Lytton but

No camera phone can truly capture the
Lynnwood Ridge but

no painting can leaden protest of one's home but

no your safety is for my fences but

no my Engineering Department could paint
something better than that but

no I own three cars and rode on the bus once but

no I own the corny romance of the frontier but

No the Hub Oil explosion never happened but

no I goosed my income by tasting a little of
everything but

no there isn't a natural process cheap enough for
real estate but

no these cedars are way too sensitive to
changes in light but

no that junk shot fired into the leak made for
great media strategy but

no I've never betrayed my CEO but

No length of toxic plume will flower into 400
Olympic-sized swimming pools but

no amount of heat will boil the Athabasca
River but

no I won't worry when waterskiing across it but

no I don't find Tintern Abbey beautiful but

no I'm talking as an investor but

No we don't ever get to see the impact of our
lives in aggregate but

no we've all walked through the forest and
really tried to attenuate but

no we've forested the planet with what deep
geological time intended but

no I don't identify as a natural resource
economy per se but

no I put schools in mines and factories too but

no I'd rather get an aerial shot of Lac-Mégantic
not happening but

No I parked my car by the lake where we shared
a bottle of wine but

no the maples are about all stripped of leaves
now but

no the birches are not rich in colour but

no I'd have deep water and a horizon but

no I'd replace lost land with new land by filling
open pit mines with water but

no I'd be a duck too busy navigating the air
currents but

no Base Mine Lake looks like any other lake in
Athabasca from a distance but

No we have decades of research that makes us
horny to test at this scale but

no we won't be able to submerge Stanley Park
to a depth of three metres but

no can you do thirty but

no there's going to be pressure to extract all
of it but

no way we're fucking waiting for spring melt

Field Guide

If I promised you a guide

to life in the twenty-first century

I'm sorry I failed you

when it didn't appear

you waited in the tailings

in the extraction fields

where geographies change daily

and floods rent everywhere

you without a life jacket

when the tide comes in

wet with delights

you can hardly bear

a balloon in a bird's gut

a faux volcanic eruption

a series of clouds seeded

with debt to investment

but when the tide retreats

you're a pop bottle poured out

stuck at the sink with capital

scrubbing your bits and drills

you frack for everything

that moulds the surface

of your kitchen countertop

no chipped paint on the cabinets

no more cracks in the tile

Audubon sketches you

facing down the A/C

because it's hot

and this is where you live

after you're done

nothing will die again

your utopian hands

will hold in

fellowship's misspilled paperwork

and any troubles

along the heart of feeling

those little kindnesses

like the thought that all

this history is going somewhere

will only remember the pleasure

of the walk between Main and Cambie

between Kingston and Queen

across 16th or along 17th

trading bald tires

for worn soles

to circumscribe

the freeway sweepstakes

of a logistical life

whose ticking mileage

measured in blocks

is never more than one

but never less than a thousand

little flowers in their little beds

won't behold deep secluded form

some species are migrants

other species scorch the territory

describe territory as progress

describe progress as everything

but in the beginning

your hands fold in

a calm shipping terminal

to inaugurate a straightforward wish

to press your face deep into the grass

to press your tongue deep into the dirt

to press to the root of love

a romantic diorama

winding pipelines through

all of this intelligible world

how do you move

the mood

when affection leads you on

when you think you can describe your feelings

you fight to forget territory

laying out a vast banquet of compliance

a sleight of hand meant

to refuse realism

no, *ref*use

swings your telescope down

to own all your runoff

all your compositional methods

your weaving eyes

your metric speech

your pale index

breathes through fracture

rather than kinship

huffing Jefferson's faith that

extinction is a myth

and nothing vanishes since

'every race of animals

received from their Maker

certain economies of nature

no instance permitted any one race

of her animals to become extinct

no, this animal still exists

in the northern and western parts

adding the light of a taper

to that of the meridian sun

no, this animal

transplanted unfriendly climates

into its fences

as rock grows in layers

and as the branches of trees

grow in every direction

the annihilation of any species

so unexampled in any economy

the bones exist therefore

nature is a never-ending circle

no, this animal species

put into a train or motion

probably still moves in that train'

a lot of things are moving

and it's hard to see what halts

your great chain of animacy

other than a small secreted tendency

to choreograph discovery

by stacking lens on lens

into a cracked panorama that

subtly anchors your chain

to a lovely water testing

caked into drainage basins

where a bright sun coaxes the banks

to the banks coaxially

you don't want to represent harm

to reproduce extinguishment

but do want to extinguish reproduction

to stop elimination

but not stop stoppage

you try to remember what Trudeau says

'we must forget many things

if we want to live together'

but your cuffs are wet with all this crisis

crisis is one word that pools

crisis tides over and over

crisis wells up in this report

crisis settles in the banks

crisis is a word that settlers use

crisis is the word you use

because you're a settler

but who is the crisis

just look at your paycheque

signed in the name of crisis

didn't crisis pay your rent

didn't crisis spring for groceries

crisis bulwarks against denial

stabilizing the dam

by ignoring the leak

rather than hand-wringing over the leak

in advance of filling it

rather than destroying the dam

which will swell the river

out into a kind of harm too

isn't the dam part of the land now

aren't the pipes that run through

the city's complicated infrastructures

part of the river now

isn't the river

pumped into your toilet

where you shit into the river

and its modernist filtration asks

how do you resolve crisis

by filtering out the ways

your shit is part of the crisis

because someone drinking your shit

somewhere downriver

is just a metaphor

you say

but that metaphor travels downstream

while you sniff your own asshole

discover its material

then ask your mirror

what about your family

what about your friends

who depend on that job

that tar and that logic

that assumption habitat exceeds

that advances class to accelerate ease

with a provincial comportment

that you say is the province's jurisdiction

when the province makes a fiery speech

instead of dealing with the province's fires

but you take a deep breath and

you look out your window

to try to forget

it's not so smoky

so long as you're inside

you reach for your phone

frame the shot carefully

caption it #myhiroshima

the gentle breeze and blue sky

spring smell of sakura

cherry notes to the sun

now trending on Instagram

a small secret tendency

to frame discovery

in terms of ownership

you say

no one owns it

this landscape that no one owns

and because no one owns it

it's a landscape that no one owns

no one patented this landscape

because you discovered that

no one owns anything

except for you

in the smoke

you put on your yellow vest

parade your F-150

through your version of pride

take a long drag

of a bird burned from books

hawks banked in the slow

bourgeois flap of gulls

nothing vanishes

is gone ever

you raise your sign

into a reactionary account

a shell history of gunfire

the law's charred folly

a long chain of crisis

you shoot from the train window

catalogues a range of ghosts

that worship the stump

gold and brass turn

dates forward

from the stump of a mast

ghost shape of the tree

dawns a coat of arms

water stretched checklist

your ankles magnetized

to the data in these forests

your skin a coyote's tail

wound around a telegraph line

stories recount the sky

accounts of the tamed sun

as its urbanizing grid

mouths estuaries out

to ship each car to market

slurry oozing ancient

meal to the body

a kind of neighbourlessness

treading through the quadrat

of your renovated kitchen

no glimpse of the timberline

observes the passing hands

of the densifying city

but if you set the frame right

that frame is exactly

a set of patents

to increase your easement

you walk through the woods

to observe all your pleasure

collect all these frames

to slide out of weather

your cautious rhythm

a degraded habitat

an imploded hospital in the sky

over the natural fantasy

you opt to occupy

what's that sectional cost

the cost of what new aesthetic

a passenger pigeon–shaped hole

a series of luxury condos

along the downtown waterline

the buzz of life

good at sorting garbage

paper in a yellow bag

cans in a blue bin

everything onto a boat

capsized into the ocean

a city in space

better than sorting garbage

into the rays of each billing caress

what's the reward for sorting yourself

past the hand of congestion

outdoors in the wheat

but in the footsteps of your last waking glance

you try a story that shreds story

you learned in a seminar

a cheat sheet deserializing need

first, live without water

then oxygen

then carbon

no ethics

no aesthetics

no dispersal

no demand

just a deterritorializing wave

of a million hands wishing you

some good news down the chyron

'when I love how eco-celebs meet

to decide the fate of the little people

I adore the buttercups

who pray that temps hold

their souls like a thermostat'

oil pours from your eyes

so that your children won't know to finance

they'll bet on quick changes

and a diet proving only

that no one will need to live without disease

each of them will dream of a slow swim to burial

a dream whose price is a textbook's disapproval

but that's hypothetical

you're not having any kids

and you received $10,000

from the Canada Council for the Arts

to write a book titled *Field Guide*

that would grapple with extinction

by writing around it

each poem an entry

for an animal made extinct

during the Anthropocene

a word you won't learn for three more years

that marks a social contract

for the uneven distribution

of environmental burden

you threw those poems out

they were a magic trick at best

a waste of time at worst

because of their lack of alarm

and a turn in your thinking

and now here you are

awash in urgency

writing this poem titled "Field Guide"

trying to salvage something

from all that wasted time

but what have you accomplished

you can't drink salt water

you can't live in a desert

you can't live in the fiction

that settlement patterns are cyclical

that a clutched cameo makes one step

your covered mouth another

and when the cloud comes in the night

and the Earth finally gets its revenge

you'll make an impassioned stampede

northward and westward

until you form the far-tossed spray

of that monstrous flood

no man is an island

you hear that somewhere

but across your island

your panic hardens

your scattered clusters

into a wall of bodies towered into the ocean

your illuminated centuries of evolution

brush the lens of its pestering dust

to document an outpost for blame

on the continent of human predation

that unweaves your colonial honeycomb

if you don't settle the sun

the sun is a place to start settling

you stare into the horizon as it sinks

and think

'you need fossil fuel

when the sun ain't goin' nowhere'

imagine the sun rising on a nation

you didn't know was there

before a court ruling remembered something

something that didn't die

didn't fit a stereotype that you found

in your Dad's box of Louis L'Amour

'I never had much

but I've got enough sense to know

that a place doesn't stay nice

without you keep it so

it takes a deal of work to build a place

and a deal of work to keep it up'

so much stability

in your place-based poetic

how do you make anywhere

when you also hold everywhere together

you want some roadmap to decolonize

without self-annihilation

so you nod to the mirror

when George Manuel writes

'They would have to carry on their quest

and discover their own relationship

with the land, the water, and the animals

until the Creator gave them their own song.

But it would have to be a song

that they could sing to their own people.

They would have to do more than discover

their own song. They would have to discover

a ceremonial situation in which the song

could be given and received

within the same spirit.'

(Manuel, 1974)

George Manuel is writing about you

isn't he

about your attempt to learn a song

that doesn't accelerate to the key of death

your cells magnetized

to a crisis constantly unfolding

every overstretched moment of self-care

into a walk onto the land

where the land is a series of development decisions

driven by the actions of real estate

under the axioms of settler colonialism

and the labour relations of white supremacy

shaped by the genre of humanity

you begin to walk

until your calves hurt

stop dead in your tracks

you scan the ground for information

hey you

sapling growing through the sidewalk

how are you living in the twenty-first century

the sun is still here

though isn't it hotter

and how does water get through that concrete

your seed travelled here somehow

what do you thank for that

where do you look in a world without blame

when history is an exploded field

ripe with subsets of flight

a continental shelf caught up in your body

shivered deep into your soil

underneath the supportive sentences

of synchronized logistical chains

you praise the tendered supply

chains of intimate transmission

that predate your trade in characteristics

whose song is this

who can you teach it to

what little bird carries your refrain

when you remember to listen

something in the discourse

makes for a fine texture

to paper the drawing room

just above the specimen cabinets

the work of genealogy

maybe you call it preservation

maybe you call it scholarship

maybe you call it training

maybe you call it design

maybe you call it engagement

maybe you call it love

pull out any drawer:

Laughing Owl

(*Sceloglaux albifacies*)

'If one opens a pocket,

it may be picked.

The coins may tickle

the folds of the mantle,

edged with snow that

melts with a thought.

A melancholy stroll

marks the mewling notes

of fabric as it shifts.

A drifting rain weeps

in an accordion's drawl.

From a distance then,

one scene unfolds across

the frame of another.

Accommodates new population

that chokes up the rest.

The past deposits little

that stands firm in storms.

None in a pair turn blind.

None fold in the shag of sight.

One must carefully tease

the thread of outbound saddles

following the rutted path.

One must peel back

vivid hues at the summit

to confirm one's faint waste.

One must keep vigil.'

now try another:

Falklands Island Wolf

(*Dusicyon australis*)

'A curtain made from

modern times that one

hangs in one's window,

carefully stitched

to hold to the floor,

meat to meat.

Like islands are archipelagos,

each target scatters only

when bounded by water.

One must desperately

sneak into the tents of men

to drag their lures to one's own.

A trail of surveillance

slouches back to the ocean,

the last unexplored wild,

dense weight at its side.

One's home is a secret trap.

It keeps one's pupils small,

only speculatively seeping out.

Eventually, one turns traditional

in the way pale greens

gut each other's sets

alight whatever curtains

cover these islands.'

here you tease out a melody

waiting in the private abandon

of a statistical trace

you wait for something but

you don't know vigil's cost

the comfort of a mouth

like the mouth of a river

when you wait to speak

you wait near the ballast

wait near the drawing board

wait inside the lobby

as alarm lobbies the cost

of your vigil's shallow current

one's last word one's first

shallow heel scheduled

mouth of a husbanded bubble

but you don't want to let go

of what you've held onto

you sit in the window

of whatever Starbucks this is

one frame unfolding

across the scene of another

as the Climate Strike passes

because you can't take crowds

and have a history of panic attacks

in those unpredictable events

or something like that

really you're just scared

though you *should* be filled with existential dread

for the 25% of Canada

Trudeau says he's going to preserve

by planting two billion trees

around the pipeline he bought

you watch with the curtains open

as you huddle your decisional meat

into the arch of a historical record

information melts when you zoom in

to pan and shovel

to quarter and correction

to quarry and tar

to your shallow waiting

a kind of cowardice

but also an effect of structure

of what you've held onto

and what you want to break from

you ask whether you can separate

from the body you help form

you turn up the screens in the War Room

watch the returns pour in

while you reload the militia rifles

prepare to build a wall

and make Québec pay for it

you watch with the curtains closed

so you can't see the strikers outside

let them eat cuts

you cry from the balcony

and the crowd sells its guillotine for scrap

hanging hope on your booming promise

for a renewed boom

your aggrieved rhetoric wakes

the dormant spirits

of Manning, Aberhart, and Klein

who sing out over the stampede

'Don't cry for thee, Athabasca.

The truth is oil never left you'

what song is this

that dreams of stability

while so much just flies off

you ask a sapling

how it lives in the twenty-first century

but that sapling is a literary device

some vague gesture to the frame's edge

to Wordsworth and Tintern Abbey

to the smug condescension of nature poetry

and the smugger materiality of ecopoetry

you don't want any of these

but do want to walk through your neighbourhood

to wander under the canopy

and think about the uneven distribution of light

from Le Corbusier's utopian redesign

of cities around sunlight

to the way bourgeois streets

are lined with trees

isn't shade just another scarce resource

in the ongoing climate wars

you read about on Gizmodo

Chennai's run out of water

4.65 million people live there

'reservoirs into muddy splats

mix desalinization plants

water by train and truck

shifts the hydrological cycle

only rain can save Chennai

not nearly enough to reverse

overdrived withering

baking in drought

with weak planning'

city on the edge of a crater

how do you live in the twenty-first century

you ask

taking a sip of San Pellegrino

through a straw you just banned

because a straw is a kind of pipeline

you can ban without letting go of something

you blow cotton

across a field of lithium-ion

can you write about something

without also creating a desire for it

or does writing the poem

add a critical distance

allowing you to reflect

on your own reflection

after it seems to disappear

in the funhouse mirror

tightening your grip

around yourself

you toss and turn

dreaming of how your bed

'is part of everyone else's bed

even as your bed is denied

to others by an elaborate system

of fences and passport-checking booths'

(Spahr, 2005)

if this poem is a guide

only to the distance

between you and you

how do you measure

three metres between trees

along this section of Queen St.

13,368 km between here and Chennai

a couple blocks between here and the lake

will you drink from this lake

before it dries up too

will you toss your vape

into the crater

and call it structure

matter might be immortal

but these combinations aren't

sometimes you find that emergence reassuring

hopeful even

and other times the idea

that everything is in collapse

gets to you

but why do you get to feel bad

when you find two expired cartons of milk

to pour into the toilet

what else do you pour into that river

when your poetry becomes a font of affect

rather than a thread of thought

you share with someone

Erin Manning's question

when she quotes Whitehead

'In fact life itself is

comparatively deficient

in survival value.

The art of persistence

is to be dead."

(Whitehead, 1929)

life isn't still

though sometimes you want it to be

that weird unpredictability

tough in the touchfields of speculative pragmatism

though tact can amount to a badge

slammed down on a desk

you try to hum along

to some kind of reconciling melody

but find a welling anger

when your train is cancelled

because someone's blocking it

though you don't get why

your pulled-out baton

won't amount to any kind of reasoning

when you're just trying to get along

just long enough to pump yourself

through the abstracted space

of whatever's assembling just over there

might as well be a rock

alive for sixty million years

when the world ends

rock will be here

freed from extraction but still

in relation to whatever's left

of the climate cycles

and the gravity relation

the sun will always shine

until it doesn't

but its matter will stick around

recombine into something else

all of this matter will find another way to live

but you won't

instead you walk the ravine

past successful couples

and their structurally viable intimacies

their off-leash dogs

scoff at ravine law

rejecting the state signage

'attention coyotes

coyotes have been reported in this area

coyotes are often found

in ravine areas in Toronto

so avoid the ravine between dusk and dawn

when coyotes come out

don't turn your back on a coyote

shout in a coyote voice

throw that voice at the coyote

and keep your fucking dog on a leash

coyotes love your dog and its shit

so don't let your dog shit in the ravine

and don't let your dog interact with coyotes

your dog might become a coyote'

but doesn't the sun through the canopy

make a lovely frame

this urban park argues

that nature's still kicking

and you can fold it back into its drawer

once you're done with it

muddy creek a respite

in all that sprawl

relation's a kick

when you can leave it

the coyote's frisson

a possible thrill

a spooked musculature

bones leap from your body

in the way a library might

failed texts leap into your branches

their reportage too faint

when denial unbuckles

cost from its seat

you station your body

where the street always flows

until it doesn't

you reason that Earth

could decide to orbit

a different sun

taking a line of flight

that leaves everything dead

you fear you'll transform

back pressed against the glass

aware of your surroundings

slowly backing away

to an area of activity

backstitching everything

you make contact with

why wouldn't you love

all this unruliness

unless you're worried about your body

about your body's composition

its consistency and porosity

in a series of photographs

taken at the boundary of your body's

slat-fenced toothiness

Wayfair's exclusive deal to sell beds

to your alerted posture

Dell's contract to sell the computers used

to police your cell walls

evidence of your itchy skin circulates

on Twitter and Facebook

you break out in cages

and the hardening repose

of concentration camps

that arrest everyone moving

out of the shadow of your footprint

you write about porosity

and the gauzy potential of osmotic movement

passed at the limned edge of your hyphen

but what about all the folks

pushed up against the border

between demarcations of the human

in the difference between person and population

that you keep insisting on

sometimes everyone is subtweeting

about something you don't know

because you couldn't accept

whatever you were craving

all the ocean's spectacle

slouches toward Tokyo

New York in the remake

you slouch into your chair

jacked into your mech

spectate the grand event

the logistics of a real Godzilla

made up like a transcendent force

so you can fight on behalf

of all those drawers back home

filled with specimens

from all the buildings you stomped

you saved them

you kept them alive

at your memory's edge

pulled at your sword

to make another distinction

fetishizing your own immanence

plastic comes from your body

you love to feel it return

if you love it don't let it go

makes a definition of totality

for the twenty-first century

an important task you keep putting off

a planet is being destroyed

and besides

look at the reviews of *Chernobyl*

maybe it's worth signing up for HBO

for all that catharsis

you lived through that

you'll live through this

all that spectacle preferable

to the real violence

at the borders of your fort

you contain the Angels

that fuel your body's expansion

the fortress-city Tokyo-3 protected

by the destruction of those Angels

incommensurable to its development vision

your body oriented by this double logic

that stabilizes whatever life you want

by reorganizing the possibility-spaces

of all this other life

why give all this up

why tell spectacle what to do

when you don't have to carry the weight

of your own material assembly

just bend with the weather

or let it bend with you

take your iodine pills

after testing the dust

caked against the windows

lock the gates

against the bullet hell

just passing through

you've been out before

and this time it's much safer in

listening to the way Kate Bush rhymes

plutonium with every lung

it doesn't get too hot here

so long as you make friends with the A/C

tuck into your draft

the first heat event of the season

that upswings the temperature

between the cooling stations

laid out on the city's online map

a continuous path between spray parks

across Metro Toronto

your new mode of urban exploration

looks for the hidden pockets of cold air

folded into the entropies

of the traffic in the street

you canter where you please

teeth on the eve of activity

ease in a seized advance

your perfect weather is evidence

of 7500 years of human predation

what's the insect on this window

and why isn't it dead yet

farming footholds the soil

renders the bloodthirsty dull

you saved the Amazon in the 90s

even if it *is* still on fire

and what about this rural crime

all its ties to oil's low price

that your tongue pushes deeper into the ground

to call out your friends' non-traditional models

the supposed state of things

has a radiocarbon date

set as long or short as necessary

to make the city's amenity

land right at your feet

instead of across town

and besides

where is the climate change

when it's been snowing in the summer here

as long as the sun has shone

you scratch your button nose

rub your coal eyes

ice across your teeth

hasn't DiCaprio heard of a Chinook

even as your body melts

the heat map of the city

structures your adventure

bike along the seawall

hike along the boardwalk

that breeze off the water

that scent of colonial governance

comes off a surveying rod

through the eye of the sentient jellyfish

threatening the Canadian flag

but swallowed whole by

a geostrategy as confident as

a new bench in a national park

you sit and change

into the dress you've carried

up this mountain

where the air makes for a clearer snapshot

you look for the angle

that excludes the queue

muscling up Everest

with a song that will be sung

for a hot minute

you go to the hills

when your heart is lonely

you know you will hear

what you've heard before

a dialectic exchange around freedom

stitched into a combination of pixels

as true as the relation they capture

but that's the cynicism talking

or the sound of music

flaring up into a set of mounted antlers

jaw agape and antique

uniform migratory herds

glacial slime mould

thick demolition

shores distribution maps

faint watercolours

of border intensification

a magnificent language

racing the action of the Red River

cheap wood in a barrel-type heater

you beat your chest into an engine

that mobilizes public opinion

in the amber dim of cottage country

feathers ground into a broach

pinned to the delicacy of your crest

you park near the bridge

listen to the seed predation

roll up the windows

as your huge murder settles

on a series of plumed brushes

the cars parked underneath

title your sunsetting control

a failing bruin print

in the next auction lot

summer clouds

$1,035,000

value is bleeding value

and you feel salty

no matter what

you're friends with everyone

or you need to be

to anchor yourself to an exchange

of secondary relationships

in the heat of summer

when you flee to your cottage

set up your easel

and hang up your flag

you rock on the porch

rifle in hand

and write in a book review

'What if nature poetry

critically addressed

its own whiteness?'

you attentively frame

all the beautiful territory

that you're threatening

'The pond has dropped a foot

over the summer; / you couldn't

pole a punt across it now'

(Donlan, 2018)

the doubt in those summer clouds

circulates a wrong but very real

plastic over the lake

a paraxodical vapour

destroying labour conditions

to create more jobs

that you push in and out of your lungs

as you reminisce

into the spatial fetish of urban sprawl

you nail that junction into the stud

run that wire through the ceiling joists

across a block of empty lots

at least you're not shingling the roof

though you still give yourself a headache asking

how the fish deal with this heat

you fish through the medicine cabinet

it's okay to ask for help you say

but why is crisis the only mode

you can use to build relation

this taps into something

but as soon as the breeze clicks on

a kind of ocean currency

oscillates from the fan

should you clean out the fridge

before ordering in new groceries

how much food waste

does that action produce

a sapling right in your stomach

so you need to swallow light

when your window is a predator

do you need to smash that window

to feed whatever's in your gut

as a way of playing that hunch

until it trunks from your mouth

as a line of thinking

chunked onto the sidewalk

a tangled mass

of wipes and congealed fat

bored out of the sewers

used to think that poetry

was useful for modelling crisis

but anything else is more effective

than the affective potential of writing

could poetry help you think with instead of feel with

how do you think with the lake

when the lake hasn't been so forthcoming

hard to be generous

when the lake won't learn English

don't swim in the lake

unless you want to get sick

the lake tells you to fuck off

but what did you ever do to the lake

throw your hands up

you didn't do that shit

that you just swallowed

you only mutated

your segmented eyes

poured sand from their population

your feral cells

combed their subfossil records

with airborne toxins

so much that your surface

is now saturated with data

only distinguished in its curlicues

all this poetry can model crisis

but why would you want it to

when your nomenclature's embroidery

opens with a champagne breakfast

coronet calls from the ozone

bows to the ornate puppets

racing birds on bicycles

you can play croquet

in the inner ring

visit the VR tubes

watch your frail shell weep

on a stirring walk

through the gowns and jackets

as the environmental dial flips from

Mexican beach to African savannah

why just last time cycle

the city's band played a rousing overture

to its great founder Jeff Bezos

but outside the station

it's cold and weightless

as if a fishing net

emptied the whole ocean

your drones constantly

return from the planet below

your full fist slamming

into the warehoused surface

what did you order

fulfilled by planetary labour

a little card in the brushed aluminum cradle

your order fulfilled by you

only one implacable straw

in a series of swept corners

how unfulfilling

the shifting baseline memories

their insurgent caches of refined steel

your ravine conserved

in the holographic arcades

made possible by the reference data

in your endless drawers

more subtly gentle

than the other exhibits

dedicated to the infrastructures

of the utopian city spaces

of nineteenth-century Paris

or twentieth-century New York

largest in the data set

like a gun shot into the air repeatedly

you find it easy to understand

just how even these cities were

how they met the needs of everyone

in no way structured

around the appropriation of land

or the exploitation of labour

everyone there had a place to live

and enough to eat

but you *felt* something

walking through the ravine

but you don't know what action

comes after all of that feeling

you feel a century of trees uprooted

swept into the base of a dam

but if you really felt them

pressure your body into oil

you could understand the whole cycle

of boom-bust resource extraction

your tongue wants to go deeper

into Premier Kenney's mouth

'Alberta is open for business

to our investor confidence

unleashing a message to deregulation's

deep state enterprise

blocked in and pinned down

to a dignifying obsession with work

and a bottleneck of pent-up energy

that demands transaction

held captive by foreigners

wanting to landlock our energy

wanting to block

our unity

with all these divisive barriers

to trade mobility

that abandon markets

to foreign success

in the zero-sum game

of economic nationalism

Albertans love nature

so much we want to innovate it

this is what humans do

and besides

how do you heat your home

didn't you drive here

that fuel didn't come from nowhere

you fucking hypocrite'

(Notley, 2019)

but aren't you well behaved

when the bright sun drives you

to jump out of the water

and flop about in the mud

the tattoo in your ear

smells of crab apple and plum

your cherry notes to the sun

kiss through the green-certified windows

would a hypocrite break the ground

of their own chest to plant a garden

what flowers will you plant

marigolds would make a strong crank

powered by the chlorophyll

abraded by your teeth

your biomass becomes a brusquely dispensing crater

motorized by the winnowing mood of winds

that waste your ribcage into a budgeting delta

you wind between towering rebar

scavenge an arrow through a seeker's eye

before holograms reveal your

leaks in the shoreline

redistribute you across you

flood bearing at your waste chamber

until a budget crunch

leaves your heart fallow

ghosts in your airway

as capital moves on to your kidneys

or something like that

your organ model assumes

your body won't function

if any part disappears

newsflash

a lot has disappeared since you were born

and everything seems to work fine

but maybe that's just where you are

when you can't see all of yourself

in this historical movement

sounds like somebody needs

some social realism

you insisted in 2003

right after Trump's inauguration

the invasions of Afghanistan and Mexico

the extraction of Guantanamo

the mass deregulation of interrogation

the oilwells on fire in the ocean

the junk shots into the desert

the omnibus warfare

the drone laws

in the teenage years of the twenty-first century

you've longed for Obama's Parliament

so much better than Harper's White House

creating a scientist-shaped hole

in the city's skyline

the sky saturated with

enough pulverized science to blot out

the sun at midday

but Prime Minister Obama

he gave back all of the land

to the respective nations

who live in what we used to call Canada

he stepped down from office

retiring to make fun of Drake

for his antics at all those

Tkaronto Raptors games

against their crosstown rivals

the Scarborough Bluffs

hasn't a lot driven you

in these past two decades

you know that you know

a lot about history

and its panoramic scale

so you yell across the table

for someone to pass the gravy

you broke the wishbone

and brought the turkey back to life

taking food out of your own mouth

because that's economics, right

when distribution bottlenecks

just pop the cork

at the top of the globe

just a problem of logistics

and endless regulatory hurdles

the dialectics will muddy

when you land at street level

though in an inflationary market

it's cheaper to just be depressed

in this basement you live in

you just want to plant something

on the outskirts of the water's surface

less a sea of troubles

than a rising water line

slouching to a safer ecosystem

the ocean wants out of the heat too

so you lower a dome over the water

and inch the ocean out with a straw

what's the word for the space

found inside that straw

its crevice a landscape

rigged to dissolve

when you zoom too closely

you offer the thought bubble

floating over your head

as the necessary real estate

to solve all border problems

on this small island

viability is a sign of fate

and nature is an exquisite system

brilliantly realigning itself

into newly elegant combinations

this island infinitely expands

a net into overheating fraternity

you dip a ladle into the cool stream

and find its story refreshing

as it slowly expands its banks

into a continent of flushed wipes

you hope to drink that geography

knowing the water's cool atoms

come together to make you

but what could you make from them

designed in Calgary, written in Toronto

'what is there beyond knowing

that keeps calling to you'

(Oliver, 1992)

later as you sketch the overheating habit

of the kidneys' desert

you load up the shipping containers

until the ocean chains their supply

into a static fetish

didn't Audubon halt all those birds

so he could fix their detail

Edward Curtis and his photographs

of the verge of extinction

accelerating genocide

'so they wouldn't move

and spoil the sitting'

(King, 2003)

a storm blows out

the light of viability's merit

what direction do you swipe

to best flirt with solidarity

but marry scarcity

when you slurry back into the river

under current regulatory regimes

you want everyone to know you care

as you pour from your mouth to feed the lake

and from your own mouth you drink yourself up

as a bird disappears into the rafters

of your libidinal satisfaction

'making something disappear isn't enough

you have to bring it back'

you remove your top hat

smear on your pancake makeup

your silence-based evidence

relishes the financial models

of the climate science misrepresentations

ground into your hot dog

what do you call a society

where those extinct animals

tip to your ringleader routine

you're as funny as a cry for help

your nose blown red by the sun

lighting a cigar with the cellophane on

reposed on the galaxy-brain plays

of your liberal centrism

you'd build a time tunnel

back to whenever

daddy calls you a bad baby

who deserves a punch in

your jack boot legibility

rubbing your weak gaze

on function's mascot

a trespassing statistic

scooting back its ass on the carpet

to rewind clown back to conqueror

from Falstaff to fungiblity

your only charm

forgotten poolside

in the abandoned chill

of a final phase

your tongue dams the river

silt settles on it

you talk about timelessness

but you'll settle for

the apex of local veneer

rock grinding rock

that the wind won't budge

you wonder what will be

the moment when the soil

rises up like a wave

to bury you

you drag streams on the tile

mud bottoms the grout

pallet knife pushed under

the lino glued to the hardwood

pour boiling water under

to dissolve the glue

holding your surface down

you bulldoze any surplus

to keep the bottom clear

to shrink the city

whose pelagic space

folds and layers

your domestic sphere

into its threatening posture

yet the slowing logistics

have no suitable habitat

will planting milkweed help

you stand in your city's

commodity shortages

ask how big a rapture would need to be

to decolonize what's left

as you cut that infrastructure funding

that you deeply depend on

when the Bow floods again

it'll creep into Sunnyside

you'll find it in your kitchen

and you'll tail into the current

swim as long as you can

in the fluid shifts

of someone else's masterpiece

'In the morning

the dust hung like fog,

and the sun was as red

as ripe new blood'

(Steinbeck, 1939)

all this individualist silt

all this governing muck

all this presiding bitumen

wades into each blue heron

that echoes through

your desperate bailing

and your sandbagging cuffs

what do you call

the beginning of a geopolitical apocalypse

based in your desire

to learn to stop worrying

and make love to the sprawling crater

you leave in the side of your body

because when you erase the diagram

you drew to explain the answer to yourself

you can still see that drawing

flit from canvas to canvas

a kernel that won't decompose

whose activity can't be digested

if it belatedly feels like you dropped a bomb on yourself

that's only because you were the only place left

to grind up and inhale

to slurp bullet back to muzzle

ignoring the smash of mastheads

the landed roots of mastery

you flip through the discards

scratching at the bark of scrap

in the smoke flocking the city

but you forgot your bag at home

and you don't want to load up

another shipping container

with your heavy breathing

you huff up at the sky

hip deep in the tailings

you don't want to think

that your work in this waste

defies the weight of heaven

but you detach the legal category of land

from the surface of the earth

you float up

into all that real estate

and finally you own something

as far away from the city

as any other suburb

turn to the north

to look at the mountains

turn to the south

to look at the lake

you wish this landscape

would be specific for once

the ancient mystery

of whatever this land is

few know what it was once called

because most are racist

and benefit from a racist system

this includes you too

and you're sorry

but that doesn't count for much

when you're down to eighteen months

not even to fix things

but to stop things from getting worse

against all evidence

you believe you've got one last act

one last quarter to plug into the slot

but even if you learned a song

that didn't hurtle you to the end

you'd also need to learn to harmonize with yourself

instead you've learned to keep the frame tight

when you point your camera outward

at the right angle you'll erase

all those condos on False Creek

the traffic on the 401 during rush hour

the crest over Glenmore heading west

you'll post that photo everywhere

you want to remember

and you'll hold it up

laid on top the horizon forever

because the art of persistence

is to stay alive

isn't it

and you have to believe

that you're alive

because you deserve it

don't you

not because of a trick of history

or a series of tricks

played on someone else

and despite all that

imagine ending everything

with a trick

where after all

your bad behaviour

you look into the camera

lift the ideological veil

the prestige

jk lol

etc.

NOTES

Sunny Ways takes its title from Prime Minister Justin Trudeau's 2015 election victory speech where he exclaimed to a crowd of true believers: "Sunny ways, my friends! Sunny ways! This is what positive politics can do!" Trudeau references Wilfrid Laurier's tactical turn away from political sniping and toward a greater spirit of cooperation within government—a hope that the warm rays of the sun will prove more effective than the cold threat of the wind. In an 1895 speech, Laurier asks, "Do you not believe that there is more to be gained by appealing to the heart and soul of men rather than to compel them to do a thing?" There's a lot of hope in Laurier and Trudeau's shared appeal to positivity, but the more I turn this sunniness over, I find less to be hopeful about. The political hopefulness espoused by Trudeau feels potent, but can it combat the sunny ways of rising temperatures and smoke-filled cities?

The two poems that make up this book investigate the ideological frames that actively exclude those possibilities incompatible with extractive capitalism. In these poems, I tarry with negativity and doubt, inaction and passivity, false narratives and false flags. I've tried to grapple with the complex systems that make conviction difficult and complicity frictionless. I felt compelled in these poems to face a hope that seems inadequate at best and false at worst. I've faced off with the Calgarian in my heart and on my shoulder, a devil in angel's clothing, reminding me that even as I critique the capitalist and colonial actions destroying the planet, my family and many of my friends depend on their planet-destroying jobs. Sunniness has a peculiarly Calgarian flavour, both in the wide prairie sky and the way Calgarians pride themselves on being friendly and welcoming (as long as no one challenges the oil industry). In recent years, Calgary's company-town mentality has started to melt a little, though it has made the city's contradictions more, not less, apparent, as people struggle with trying to find the middle ground between admitting climate change is real and not wanting to lose their meal ticket. No one wants to be responsible for the end times; everyone needs to find ways to pay their rent.

"Hibernia Mon Amour" was originally commissioned by Daniel Zomparelli and *Poetry is Dead* magazine to coincide with an exhibition of Edward Burtynsky's work at the Vancouver Art Gallery. I was struck by the ways Burtynsky's massively scaled photographs of the Alberta Tar Sands differed from another set of photographs appearing on Instagram at the same time under the hashtag #myhiroshima. The hashtag was used by Fort McMurray residents after Neil Young compared the Alberta Tar Sands to the effects of nuclear weapons on Hiroshima, Japan at the end of World War II. The hashtagged photos shared scenic natural views, keeping any work sites or toxic sinks safely out of frame. The poem was performed at the VAG on April 22, 2014 alongside Jordan Abel, Amy De'Ath, and Rita Wong. It was subsequently published as part of a *Poetry is Dead* issue on the future in 2014. The current version of "Hibernia Mon Amour" was also recently published in Julian Day's long poem magazine *+doc*.

"Field Guide" began as an extended rumination on extinction, reflecting on what we save, what we memorialize, and what we refuse to let go of. It substantively reworks a manuscript I drafted in 2011 with support from the Canada Council for the Arts and the Alberta Foundation for the Arts. In the original manuscript, each poem was written as a guide book entry for species that had gone extinct during the Anthropocene, starting with classic examples like the dodo and the passenger pigeon before digging into an array of the recently erased. This current version of the piece was drafted between March and August 2019. "Laughing Owl (*Sceloglaux albifacies*)" and "Falklands Island Wolf (*Dusicyon australis*)" are poems from the original manuscript draft and were previously published in *The Capilano Review and Poetry is Dead* respectively. *Dandelion* magazine also published a section from this earlier manuscript on their short lived blog. "Field Guide" irresponsibly trades in a poetics of misinformation. Throughout the piece, I cite (and fail to cite) a variety of sources, not always accurately, though I have tried to be responsible in my irresponsibility. Sources include the following, in order of appearance: Chelsea Vowel's 2019 keynote "Law for the Apocalypse: ~~Order Out of Chaos~~ Kinship Out of Fracture"; Thomas Jefferson's writings on species extinction (via Mark V. Barrow Jr.'s *Nature's Ghosts* and the internet); Pierre Trudeau's remarks at a 1969 Vancouver Liberal Association dinner (via Geoff Mann's article "It Was Not Supposed to End This Way"); M.P. Shiel's *The Purple Cloud*; Amiri Baraka's "Somebody Blew Up America"; Louis L'Amour's *Over on the Dry Side*; George Manuel's *The Fourth World: An Indian Reality*; Andrew Lloyd Webber and Tim Rice's *Evita*; Brian Kahn's Gizmodo article "Why Chennai, India's Sixth Biggest City, Has Run Out of Water"; Juliana Spahr's *This Connection of Everyone With Lungs*; Erin Manning's *The Minor Gesture*, quoting Alfred North Whitehead; the City of Toronto's signage at the Kingston Road entrance of the Glen Stewart Ravine; *Godzilla*; *Chernobyl*; *Neon Genesis Evangelion*; Kate Bush's *Never for Ever*; *The Sound of Music*; Tom Thomson's *Summer Clouds*; both John Donlan's *Out All Day* and my own book review of it; Jason Kenney's 2019 election victory speech, here credited to Rachel Notley; Mary Oliver's *New and Selected Poems*; Christopher Nolan's *The Prestige*; Thomas King's *The Truth About Stories*; John Steinbeck's *The Grapes of Wrath*; and a few sources I've lost track of.

ACKNOWLEDGEMENTS

Thanks to Norm Nehmetallah, Andrew Faulkner, and Leigh Nash at Invisible for taking a risk on this pair of long poems. Thanks to Megan Fildes for her excellent book design. And many thanks to Laurie D. Graham for her thoughtful editorial feedback as we edited the book together, smoothing out and amplifying the book's assorted craggy edges.

The original manuscript of "Field Guide" was written in what feels like a different lifetime, but in 2011 I would've thanked the following people who would've shaped my thinking in one way or another: Clea Anaïs, Pamela Banting, Claudia Bustos, James Dangerous, Stephanie Davis, Laurie Anne Fuhr, Samuel Garrigó Meza, Jocelyn Grossé, Ian Kinney, L.T. Leif, Tyler Los-Jones, Marc Herman Lynch, Eric Moschopedis, David Nuñez Toews, Susan Rudy, Dana Schloss, and Katherine Ziff.

For friendship and conversation, thanks to Haida Antolick, Jonathan Ball, Chris and Sandy Ewart, Deanna Fong, Danielle LaFrance, rob mclennan, Rajinderpal S. Pal, Julia Polyck- O'Neill, Nikki Sheppy, Aaron Tucker, Karina Vernon, and you.

ryan fitzpatrick is the publisher of the online-based and poetry-focused Model Press. He was on the editorial collective of *filling Station* magazine and helped found the Flywheel Reading Series. He is the author of four books of poetry, including *Coast Mountain Foot* (Talonbooks), *Fortified Castles* (Talonbooks), and *Fake Math* (Snare Books). A former resident of Calgary and Vancouver, ryan now lives in Toronto.